EXPLORE
COLONIAL
AMERICA

BEN
FRANKLIN

Sarah Gilman

Enslow Publishing
101 W. 23rd Street
Suite 240
New York, NY 10011
USA

enslow.com

Published in 2017 by Enslow Publishing, LLC.
101 W. 23rd Street, Suite 240, New York, NY 10011

Library of Congress Cataloging-in-Publication Data

Names: Gilman, Sarah, author.
Title: Ben Franklin / Sarah Gilman.
Description: New York, NY : Enslow Publishing, 2017. | Series: Explore colonial America | Includes
bibliographical references and index. | Audience: Ages 9-up. | Audience: Grade 4 to 6.
Identifiers: LCCN 2015050571| ISBN 9780766078734 (library bound) | ISBN 9780766078796 (pbk.)
| ISBN 9780766078611 (6-pack)
Subjects: LCSH: Franklin, Benjamin, 1706-1790--Juvenile literature. | Statesmen--United States--
Biography--Juvenile literature. | Scientists--United States--Biography--Juvenile literature. |
Inventors--United States--Biography--Juvenile literature. | Printers--United States--Biography--
Juvenile literature.
Classification: LCC E302.6.F8 G475 2016 | DDC 973.3092--dc23
LC record available at http://lccn.loc.gov/2015050571

Printed in the United States of America

To Our Readers: We have done our best to make sure all website addresses in this book were active and
appropriate when we went to press. However, the author and the publisher have no control over and
assume no liability for the material available on those websites or on any websites they may link to. Any
comments or suggestions can be sent by e-mail to customerservice@enslow.com.

Portions of this book originally appeared in the book *Meet Ben Franklin* by Elaine Landau.

CONTENTS

MAP OF BEN FRANKLIN'S PHILADELPHIA 4

CHAPTER ONE
THE FIFTEENTH CHILD 5

CHAPTER TWO
A PRINTER'S APPRENTICE....................9

CHAPTER THREE
ARRIVING IN PHILADELPHIA 13

CHAPTER FOUR
A PRINT SHOP OF HIS OWN.......................17

CHAPTER FIVE
ROOM FOR IMPROVEMENT 20

CHAPTER SIX
INVENTION AND DISCOVERY 24

CHAPTER SEVEN
OFF TO ENGLAND.....................29

CHAPTER EIGHT
REVOLUTIONARY ROLES 34

CHAPTER NINE
AMERICA'S REPRESENTATIVE 38

CHAPTER TEN
AN AMERICAN HERO 41

TIMELINE 45
GLOSSARY 46
FURTHER READING 47
FOR MORE INFORMATION 47
INDEX...................48

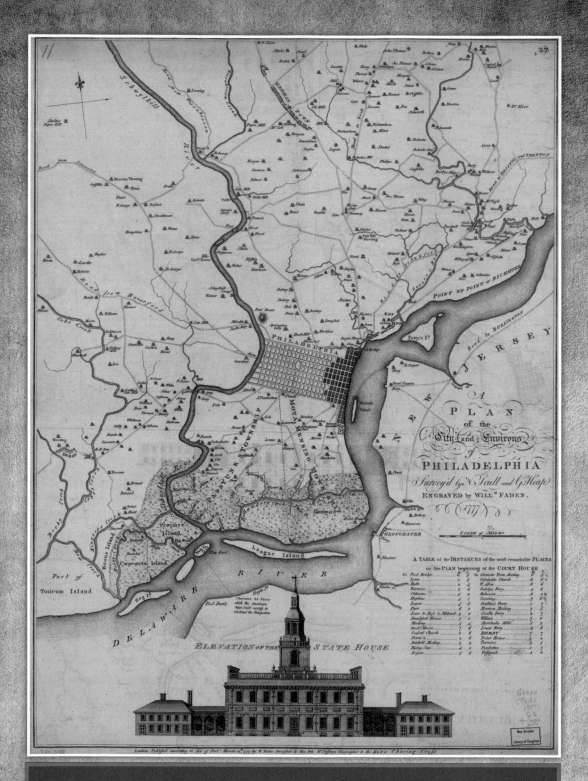

During Ben Franklin's time, Philadelphia was an important city. The bustling seaport became the meeting place of the nation's Founding Fathers.

THE FIFTEENTH CHILD

On January 17, 1706, Ben Franklin was born in Boston. That morning, Ben's mother, Abiah, had gone to Sunday service at church. She came home and gave birth to Ben. Then Ben's father, Josiah Franklin, took baby Ben to church to be christened. Ben Franklin would later say that he spent the first day of his life in church.

Ben Franklin was his mother's eighth child. His father had been married before. He had children from that marriage, too. So Ben was his father's fifteenth child. Ben was the youngest boy in the family. That made him special to his family.

The Franklins lived in Boston, Massachusetts. Boston was a growing colonial city. About six thousand people lived there. The city had a busy harbor as well. Ben's father earned a living making soap and candles.

Ben Franklin and his family lived in this house. The Franklin home was located on Boston's Milk Street. Boston would play a key role in American independence.

A BUDDING MINISTER

Ben came from a religious home. His father led the family in prayer for an hour each morning. They prayed together again in the evening.

Ben's father sent him to school to become a minister when Ben was eight. Ben was the best student in his class. Yet, within the year, his father took Ben out of the school because he could not pay for the training. After Ben left school, he studied penmanship (handwriting) and math with a teacher. He also read and studied a lot on his own.

SEEKING A TRADE

When Ben turned ten, his school days were over. In 1716, he began making soap and candles with his father. Ben did not like the work and hated the smell.

Ben's father tried to find a trade that his son would like. The two took long walks together. Ben saw bricklayers and

EXPLORE THE FACTS

A STUDENT FOREVER

Ben Franklin didn't attend school for long. However, he studied and learned for the rest of his life. Ben was filled with curiosity. That made him eager to learn new things.

blacksmiths at work. His father talked to Ben about other trades in the colony as well.

However, none seemed to interest young Ben. Instead, Ben dreamed of becoming a sailor. His father was against it. One of Ben's older brothers had gone off to sea and drowned. Ben's father wanted Ben to be safe.

Josiah Franklin knew that he had to find another trade for Ben. But what could his youngest son do? No one imagined how exciting Ben's future would become.

CHAPTER TWO

A PRINTER'S APPRENTICE

Ben's brother James Franklin owned a print shop in Boston. He put out a newspaper called the *New England Courant*. It was one of America's first newspapers.

Ben became his brother's apprentice in 1718. Young boys learned various trades this way. Apprentices worked for a tradesman for nine years. The boys were fed and given a room. However, they were not paid.

SILENCE DOGOOD

Being in a print shop suited Ben. He worked hard and learned quickly. Ben was also a good writer and loved to read. Often, he met booksellers who gave him different books. Sometimes Ben read all night.

Ben Franklin began his amazing career by working as a printer's apprentice. There, he showcased his clever sense of humor. He also learned to develop skills that would serve him well in his future role as one of America's founding fathers.

Ben longed to write for the newspaper. But his brother would never print anything he wrote. So Ben began writing under a different name. He pretended to be a middle-aged woman named Silence Dogood.

Ben wrote about all sorts of things as Mrs. Dogood. Sometimes he wrote about new clothing styles. Other times he wrote about people who drank too much. Ben sent Mrs. Dogood's pieces to the paper. James printed these and the public loved them.

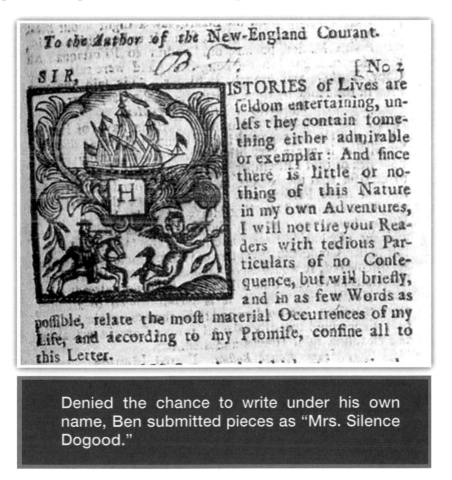

Denied the chance to write under his own name, Ben submitted pieces as "Mrs. Silence Dogood."

When James learned the truth, he was very angry. In a rage, he told Ben that he would never publish anything Ben wrote again. Nevertheless, before long, James would need his younger brother. James had to spend some time in jail for criticizing (speaking out against) the colony's government in his paper. Ben ran the paper while James was gone. He did a fine job and many people now felt the paper was funnier and better written. More people began buying it.

A HARD CHOICE

When James returned, he again took charge. Ben was supposed to go back to being an apprentice. This was difficult for Ben. He now knew that he could run the paper well on his own. He felt that he deserved his brother's respect.

However, James was not about to change his ways. He was not grateful for Ben's help. He was still often harsh and demanding.

Ben was tired of being treated this way. He was sixteen now—old enough to be on his own. But his brother made it hard for Ben to leave. James spoke to the other Boston printers. He told them not to hire his brother.

Ben had no choice. He would have to leave Boston. He sold some of his books to get a little money. Then in October 1723, Ben boarded a boat for New York.

He could not find work as a printer there. So he went on to Philadelphia. Ben was ready to start his new life.

CHAPTER THREE

ARRIVING IN PHILADELPHIA

Philadelphia was a large and exciting colonial city. In 1723, it was bigger than both Boston and New York. Philadelphia was an ideal place for an ambitious young man like Ben Franklin. It was a growing center for shipping and trade. There was a lot to see and even more to do there.

Philadelphia's busy city streets were lined with colorful houses and shops. There seemed to be people everywhere. Some sold goods while others were buying. American Indians walked the streets with animal pelts swung over their shoulders. They had come to the city to sell their pelts. Farmers came, too. They brought their chickens, milk, and eggs to sell.

Both entertainment and fashion were important in Philadelphia. All kinds of parties, dinners, and other outings were held. People wore stylish clothes and hairdos. They talked for hours in coffee shops and taverns.

During colonial times, Philadelphia was a bustling city. It also was one of the country's greatest seaports. At least twelve shipbuilding companies were located there when Ben arrived.

A FATEFUL MEETING

Franklin felt at home in this exciting city at once. But no one would have guessed that when he arrived. The boat trip to Philadelphia had been hard. At first the waters were choppy. The waves soaked the passengers. Later, there was no wind. Franklin and the others took turns rowing. He got off the boat looking wet and tired.

A young woman about his age noticed him walking down a city street that day. Her name was Deborah Read Rogers. Deborah laughed when she saw Ben. Dressed in his damp and wrinkled clothes, Ben Franklin was quite a sight.

At first, Ben was insulted. He did not like being laughed at. He walked away upset. Ben thought he would never see Deborah again. However, he couldn't have been more wrong.

After meeting Rogers, Franklin quickly settled in Philadelphia. He got a job working for a printer. He even rented a room from Deborah Read Rogers' parents. Ben soon forgot all about his first unpleasant meeting with Deborah. The two became quite close.

FRIENDS IN HIGH PLACES

People liked Franklin. Before long, he had a number of friends. They spent many evenings talking about their favorite books. Ben looked forward to these evenings out. He enjoyed exchanging new ideas with others.

Even the Pennsylvania colony's governor, Sir William Keith, liked Ben Franklin. Keith had heard that Ben was a good printer. The governor saw that Franklin was smart and hardworking. He thought that Franklin should have his own print shop. Best of all, he promised to help him get one.

Wet, tired, and messy upon his arrival in Philadelphia, Ben walked through the city streets. A young woman laughed at his appearance. This woman was Deborah Read Rogers, Ben's future wife.

CHAPTER FOUR

A PRINT SHOP OF HIS OWN

Sir William Keith offered to finance Ben Franklin's print business. He wanted Franklin to go to England to buy equipment for the shop. Franklin sailed to England in 1724. However, Keith's financing fell through.

Franklin landed in England without much money. He went to work for a printer. Over the next eighteen months, he saved enough money for his return trip home. On July 23, 1726, Franklin boarded a ship for Philadelphia. He returned without the printing equipment he had hoped to get in England.

FAMILY AND CAREER

In 1728, Franklin went into business with a friend. His friend's father was to supply the necessary money. Franklin would supply the talent and hard work. The print shop did well. People brought their work to Franklin. They knew that he would do a good job. He even printed up paper money for the colony.

Sir William Keith took a liking to Franklin. He offered to pay for his printing equipment. But the governor never followed through on the letters of introduction he promised.

In 1729, Ben Franklin also bought a newspaper. He named the paper the *Pennsylvania Gazette*. Before long, his paper earned him money, too.

That same year, Franklin bought out his partner. Now he finally owned his own print shop. Then in 1730, Deborah Read Rogers became his wife.

However, at about the same time, Franklin had a son with another woman. No one knows for sure who the boy's mother was. Some say it was a servant in the Franklin household. In any case, the boy was named William. He lived with the Franklins.

Ben and Deborah Franklin also had two of their own children. Their son, Francis, died of smallpox when he was four. Sometime later, the couple had a daughter named Sarah. Ben nicknamed her Sally.

Deborah and Ben Franklin also opened a store. They sold cloth, soap, tools, and other useful items. Deborah helped with Franklin's printing business, too. They were a hardworking and very busy couple.

Ben Franklin finally achieved his dream of opening his own printing business. He also owned a newspaper called the *Pennsylvania Gazette*, which he ran with associates.

ROOM FOR IMPROVEMENT

B en Franklin spent much of his time trying to improve himself. He made a list of good qualities in people. Among these were spending money wisely and treating others fairly.

Each week Franklin picked a trait from the list. He would try to improve himself in that area. Franklin soon found that this was not easy. Yet he kept trying.

POOR RICHARD

Franklin wished to improve things for others, too. In 1731, he and some friends helped start the first public library. Then in 1732, Ben Franklin published an almanac called *Poor Richard's Almanack*. Almanacs have weather forecasts, recipes, and helpful sayings in them. In Ben Franklin's time, "almanac" was spelled with a "k" on the end of it.

Ben Franklin believed that everyone should have access to reading materials. But at that time, books were expensive. Franklin devised the first public library. It allowed everyone the opportunity to learn.

Poor Richard's Almanack was filled was good advice. Many sayings from it are still used today. "A penny saved is a penny earned" is just one of these.

COMMUNITY PROJECTS

Ben Franklin cared deeply about Philadelphia. He wanted the city and its people to do well. So he started a lot of useful community projects.

Franklin worried about fires in the city. People often lost their lives, homes, and businesses in these blazes. In 1736, Franklin

Poor Richard, 1743.

AN

Almanack

For the Year of Chrift

1743,

Being the Third after LEAP YEAR.

And makes fince the Creation	Years
By the Account of the Eaftern *Greeks*	7251
By the Latin Church, when ☉ ent. ♈	6942
By the Computation of *W. W.*	5752
By the *Roman* Chronology	5692
By the *Jewifh* Rabbies	5504

Wherein is contained,

The Lunations, Eclipfes, Judgment of the Weather, Spring Tides, Planets Motions & mutual Afpects, Sun and Moon's Rifing and Setting, Length of Days, Time of High Water, Fairs, Courts, and obfervable Days.

Fitted to the Latitude of Forty Degrees, and a Meridian of Five Hours Weft from *London*, but may without fenfible Error, ferve all the adjacent Places, even from *Newfoundland* to *South-Carolina*.

By RICHARD SAUNDERS, Philom.

PHILADELPHIA:
Printed and fold by *B. FRANKLIN*, at the New Printing-Office near the Market.

Franklin began printing *Poor Richard's Almanack* annually in 1732. This popular newspaper offered practical advice as well as bits of Franklin's trademark humor. This is the cover of the 1743 edition of the almanac.

began the city's first fire company. He later also helped start a fire insurance company.

In 1736, Ben Franklin was elected clerk of Pennsylvania's legislature (government) as well. The following year he was appointed postmaster of Philadelphia. In time, Franklin greatly improved mail service.

THE PENNSYLVANIA HOSPITAL

But Ben Franklin did not stop there. He wanted to help the sick. So in 1751, he formed a group to start the Pennsylvania Hospital. The hospital is still there today. He also helped found the school that became the University of Pennsylvania.

Meanwhile, Ben's newspaper and printing business continued to do well. He set up partnerships with people in other colonies. These businesses did well, too.

By 1749, Ben Franklin could afford to retire early. Yet that did not mean that he would do less. Ben was about to become busier than ever.

CHAPTER SIX

INVENTION AND DISCOVERY

en Franklin's natural curiosity helped him a great deal. He liked finding new and better ways to do things. This led to his becoming a respected inventor. Some of his inventions are still used today. As early as 1743, Franklin designed the Franklin stove. A person could cook on it, but it was used mostly for home heating. The Franklin stove was an improvement over the fireplace. It gave off much more heat while using less fuel.

Franklin had always loved to swim. So no one was surprised when he invented swim fins. Swimmers would attach these "fins" to their feet. It helped them swim underwater.

USING GLASS IN NEW WAYS

Ben also really enjoyed music. He played the violin, harp, and guitar, as well as other instruments. In 1761, Franklin invented a musical instrument called the glass armonica. Ben used thirty-seven different-sized glass jars to make the armonica. He was quite pleased with his new invention. Ben described its sound as both "sweet" and "heavenly."

Others agreed with him. Ben's armonica became extremely popular. Famous composers wrote music for it. The queen of France even paid for glass armonica lessons.

Ben used glass in other ways, too. In 1784, Ben Franklin invented bifocals. Bifocals are glasses that have two lenses—one to see up close and one to see farther away.

SCIENCE STUDIES

Franklin had long been interested in science. He studied weather, different rock forms, and fossils. He was also curious about medicine. He learned a lot about germs and how diseases are spread. Harvard and Yale universities

The Franklin Stove is one of Ben Franklin's most famous inventions.

Franklin was an accomplished musician. His glass armonica became very popular. Legendary composer Wolfgang Amadeus Mozart later wrote two compositions for the instrument!

EXPLORE THE FACTS

BIFOCALS

Many of Ben Franklin's inventions were solutions to his own problems. When he had trouble seeing, he invented bifocals, eyeglasses with an upper half for seeing distance and a lower half for reading.

honored Franklin for his work. In London, the Royal Society of Medicine gave him a medal.

EXPERIMENTS WITH ELECTRICITY

Very often, Ben Franklin's different interests seemed to be endless. However, it was his work with electricity that helped him become famous. In Franklin's time, people did not know very much about electricity. They did not understand the force behind lightning. But Franklin believed that lightning was a flow of electricity.

In 1752, he proved this with his well-known kite experiment. Franklin tied a metal key to a kite's string. Then he flew the kite during a thunderstorm. According to the story, lightning struck the kite. The electrical charge from the lightning traveled down to the key. As a result, Franklin received an electrical shock.

No one knows if the experiment really happened this way. Nevertheless, people today believe that the experiment occurred, and Franklin had proved his point. Lightning was electricity.

Experts aren't sure Franklin's legendary electricity experiment really happened. It is not mentioned in Franklin's otherwise detailed records. This experiment would have been very dangerous.

CHAPTER SEVEN

OFF TO ENGLAND

As early as 1754, Ben Franklin came up with a plan to unite the colonies. This was many years before the Revolutionary War. Franklin suggested his plan at a meeting known as the Albany Congress. So Franklin called it his Albany Plan of Union.

THE ALBANY PLAN

Under this plan, the colonies would unite in order to raise taxes. These taxes would be used for defense. The British and French had started fighting in North America. If the British colonies were attacked, Franklin wanted them to be ready and strong.

Franklin used his newspaper to help make his point. He printed the first political cartoon. It was a picture of a snake cut into pieces. The pieces stood for the colonies. Under it were the words: Join, or Die.

Franklin's famous political cartoon, *Join, or Die*, was intended to bring the colonies together. The drawing has since been used throughout history for various groups and interests.

However, few people liked Franklin's idea. The colonists were not ready to unite. They feared losing control over their own colonies. Great Britain was against the plan, too. It did not want the colonists to become too strong or united. That could threaten the king's power. To Franklin's disappointment, his Albany Plan never took hold. But Franklin still stayed active in politics.

TAX REBELLION

In 1756, Pennsylvania lawmakers sent Franklin to England to discuss taxes with King George III. By 1765, a more serious problem arose in the colonies. King George III of Britain and Parliament (the British form of government) had begun to heavily tax the colonies. The Stamp Act of 1765 was one of the first taxes. It made the colonists buy government stamps to be placed on newspapers, playing cards, documents, and other items. The colonists felt the taxes were unfair. They argued that they had no one to represent them in Parliament.

The colonists refused to give in. They would not pay the taxes. They made threats toward the British tax collectors. The angry colonists also rebelled (they disobeyed either through the use of force or breaking the law) in other ways, too. They boycotted, or refused, to buy British goods.

A HOPELESS SITUATION

From England, Franklin acted as the colonists' representative. Besides Pennsylvania, Franklin was now also asked to speak for Georgia, New Jersey, and Massachusetts.

Franklin tried to work things out with the king and Parliament. He even spoke before Parliament to explain the colonists' feelings. He also wrote articles and drew cartoons on the subject.

Nevertheless, things worsened. Franklin saw that the king did not care about the colonists. King George III felt that he had a right to tax them. If they rebelled, he would use force against them.

Angry Boston citizens burned the Stamp Act. The colonists were fed up with all the taxes England was imposing on them. They felt they were being treated unfairly.

Franklin tried to find a fair way to solve this problem. But the British Parliament did not listen to him. He realized that the situation was hopeless.

Ben Franklin could not help the colonies by remaining in England. He set sail for Philadelphia on March 21, 1775. By the time he had arrived home, war had broken out between Britain and the colonies.

CHAPTER EIGHT

REVOLUTIONARY ROLES

B en Franklin's ship docked in Philadelphia on April 19, 1775. Things were not going well. His wife had died while he was away. Also, in February, colonial troops had battled the British at Lexington and Concord.

CIVIC DUTIES

Ben had little time to rest. The next morning, he was picked to serve in the Second Continental Congress. This was a congress made up of representatives from all thirteen colonies. These men had to decide what to do about the trouble with Britain. Things had not improved. The colonists had to prepare for the worst.

Now Franklin also headed Pennsylvania's Committee for Safety. The committee trained the men of Pennsylvania to fight. Later, those men would join together with other colonial soldiers to form the Continental Army.

The growing anger between the colonists and England came to a head when the first shots were fired at the Battle of Lexington. Thus began the Revolutionary War.

Ben Franklin was appointed postmaster general as well. He came up with new postal routes. The colonies needed to stay in close touch during wartime.

Franklin served on a secret committee, too. This group wrote to important people in Europe. They asked them to side with the colonists.

Thomas Jefferson composed a first draft of the Declaration of Independence. But Ben Franklin made his mark on the important document by suggesting several changes and additions.

EXPLORE THE FACTS

A SURPRISING LOYALTY

Not all colonists wanted to break from England. They were called Loyalists. One such Loyalist was Benjamin Franklin's son William. Their difference in opinion caused many arguments.

INDEPENDENCE

Ben Franklin felt that the colonies should be independent. So he also served on the committee to write the Declaration of Independence. This was important work. If the colonies voted to break away from Britain, the declaration had to explain why.

Most of this document was written by a young representative from Virginia. His name was Thomas Jefferson. However, Franklin made some important changes to it.

All the changes were approved on July 4, 1776. That day, a new nation was born. All of the thirteen colonies joined to form the new United States of America.

AMERICA'S REPRESENTATIVE

Just because the colonies had declared independence didn't mean they were free. Britain was not about to give them up. The colonists would have to fight hard for their freedom.

FINDING SUPPORT

At seventy-one, Ben Franklin was too old to join the army. So he helped in other ways. First, Franklin was sent to Canada. He asked the Canadians for help in the colonists' fight against Britain. Next, he went to France. Crossing the Atlantic was dangerous. If the British captured his ship, Franklin would surely hang. To the British, Franklin was a traitor. The trip was not easy for Franklin. His health had begun to fail. Yet, he insisted on doing his part.

Ben Franklin met France's King Louis XVI at his palace at Versailles in 1778. Franklin had been sent to France to round up support for the colonies' independence.

Though it took some time, Franklin was successful in France. Franklin was a good representative. He made many friends for the new nation. The French also began to believe in the colonists. At the Battle of Saratoga, the colonists defeated the large well-trained British army. The French were impressed by this victory. They agreed to come to the colonists' aid.

EXPLORE THE FACTS

AN AMERICAN IN FRANCE

Ben Franklin became so popular in France that his picture was put on rings, handkerchiefs, and other things. In a letter to his daughter, he wrote, "My face is as well known as the moon."

THE TREATY OF PARIS

After the colonists defeated Britain, Franklin was one of five men asked to write a peace treaty. While he was in France, he and several other men worked out the details of the peace treaty, called the Treaty of Paris.

Ben Franklin finally left France on May 2, 1785. He had been there for over eight years. During this time, he served as America's ambassador to France. The French were sorry to see him go. Franklin had become quite popular there.

Franklin was also warmly greeted when he returned to the United States. Cannons were fired to welcome him home. People were grateful for all he had done.

AN AMERICAN HERO

A month after his return, Franklin was elected head of Pennsylvania's government. He did his best to help the state. Yet his work did not end there. Franklin wanted all people to be free. He once owned slaves, but had freed them. Now he hoped to see slavery outlawed. He became president of Pennsylvania's Abolitionist Society. This group also wanted slavery made illegal.

THE US CONSTITUTION

Ben Franklin was also chosen as one of Pennsylvania's delegates (representatives) to the Constitutional Convention. These men had a difficult job to do. They would write the US Constitution. This document listed the main laws of the United States.

Members of the Constitutional Convention signed the US Constitution in 1787. These men had done a good job. The US Constitution has lasted for over two hundred years.

EXPLORE THE FACTS

ABSENT AMERICAN

For an American hero, Ben Franklin spent a lot of time out of the country. In fact, he was abroad for twenty-seven of his eighty-four years. Franklin crossed the Atlantic Ocean eight times during his life.

Now eighty-one, Franklin was the oldest delegate at the Congress. However, he did not have far to travel. The Congress was held in Philadelphia. At the time, it was the largest city in America. Franklin and the other delegates signed the Constitution on September 17, 1787.

Ben Franklin lived to be eighty-four. He died quietly on April 17, 1790. Over twenty thousand people went to his funeral. In France, a three day mourning period was declared.

Ben Franklin had been an outstanding American. His ideas were important in shaping our country. He wanted a nation where people lived as equals. Franklin felt that with hard work, anyone should be able to get ahead in the United States of America. Ben Franklin was a man who truly loved his country. He spent much of his time working for the public good. His was a life well-lived.

Though he became a famous inventor and scientist, Franklin was much more. His love of America and his dedication to improvement continue to inspire us all.

1706 Ben Franklin is born on January 17.

1716 Goes to work in his father's soap and candle shop.

1718 Becomes an apprentice in his brother's print shop.

1723 Runs away to Philadelphia to begin a new life.

1724 Leaves for England.

1726 Returns to Philadelphia from England.

1728 Goes into the printing business with a partner.

1729 Buys a newspaper that he names the *Pennsylvania Gazette*.

1730 Marries Deborah Read Rogers.

1731 Starts the first public library.

1732 Publishes the first *Poor Richard's Almanack*.

1736 Helps establish Philadelphia's first fire company. That year he is also elected clerk of Pennsylvania's legislature.

1737 Is appointed postmaster.

1743 Invents the Franklin stove.

1749 Retires from the printing business.

1751 Helps establish the Pennsylvania Hospital.

1752 Performs his famous kite experiment.

1761 Invents the glass armonica.

1775 Is a delegate to the Second Continental Congress.

1784 Invents bifocals.

1787 Franklin and the other delegates sign the US Constitution.

1790 Ben Franklin dies on April 17.

GLOSSARY

APPRENTICE—A young person who learns a trade by working with a skilled person over a period of time.

CHRISTEN—To baptize in the Christian faith.

COLONY—A settlement in a new area.

DELEGATE—A person sent as a representative to an important meeting.

DOCUMENT—A paper containing important information.

LEGISLATURE—A lawmaking body.

PARLIAMENT—A form of government in England in which representatives are elected.

PELT—An animal skin.

TAX—Money collected from people to support their government.

TRAITOR—Someone who sides with the enemy of his or her nation.

TREATY—An agreement between nations.

FURTHER READING

Coleridge, Margaret. *Who Was Benjamin Franklin?* New York: Rosen Classroom, 2013.

Crawford, Laura, and Judy Hierstein. *Benjamin Franklin from A to Z.* Gretna, LA: Pelican Publishing, 2013.

Freedman, Russell. *Becoming Ben Franklin: How a Candlemaker's Son Helped Light the Flame of Liberty.* New York: Holiday House, 2013.

Proudfit, Benjamin. *Benjamin Franklin.* New York: Gareth Stevens Publishing, 2015.

FOR MORE INFORMATION

BEN FRANKLIN—AN EXTRAORDINARY LIFE. AN ELECTRIC MIND.
www.pbs.org/benfranklin

Visit this PBS website to learn more about the remarkable civic leader and inventor—Ben Franklin.

BEN'S GUIDE TO US GOVERNMENT FOR KIDS— BENJAMIN FRANKLIN
bensguide.gpo.gov/

Learn about Ben Franklin's work as a printer, librarian, inventor, and statesman.

INDEX

A

Albany Plan of Union, 29–30
American colonies, 12, 13, 23, 29–31, 33, 34–35, 37, 38
American Indians, 13
American Revolution, 29, 33 34–35, 37

B

Battle of Saratoga, 40
bifocals, 25, 27
Boston, Massachusetts, 5, 9, 12, 13

C

Canada, 38
Constitutional Convention, 41, 43
Continental Army, 34–35, 38

D

Declaration of Independence, 37
Dogood, Silence, 9, 11–12

E

electricity, 27
England/Great Britain, 17, 29–31, 33, 34, 37–38, 40

F

fire company, 21, 23
fire insurance company, 23
France, 25, 29, 38, 40, 43
Franklin, Abiah (mother), 5
Franklin, Benjamin
    advice of, 20–21
    apprentice, 9, 11–12
    birth, 5
    children, 18–19, 37

clerk, 23
death, 43
education, 7–8
improvements to Philadelphia, 20–21, 23
inventor and scientist, 24–25, 27
politician, 23, 29–31, 33, 34–35, 37, 38, 40, 41, 43
postmaster, 23
postmaster general, 35
printer, 12, 15, 17–19, 20–21, 23
retirement, 23
self-improvement, 9, 15, 20–21, 24–25
writer, 9, 11–12
Franklin, Deborah Read Rogers (wife), 15, 18–19, 34
Franklin, Francis (son), 19
Franklin, James (brother), 9, 11–12
Franklin, Josiah (father), 5, 7–8
Franklin, Sarah (daughter), 19, 40
Franklin, William (son), 18, 37
Franklin stove, 24

G

glass armonica, 24–25
George III, King of England, 30–31

J

Jefferson, Thomas, 37

K

Keith, Sir William, 15, 17

L

Loyalists, 37

M

mail, 23

N

New England Courant, 9, 11–12
New York, 12, 13

P

Parliament, 31, 33
Pennsylvania, 15, 18, 23, 31, 34, 41
Pennsylvania Abolitionist Society, 41
Pennsylvania Committee for Safety, 34
Pennsylvania Gazette, 18, 23
Pennsylvania Hospital, 23
Philadelphia, Pennsylvania 12, 13, 15, 17, 21, 23, 33, 34, 43
political cartoons, 29–31
Poor Richard's Almanack, 20–21
public library, 20–21

S

Second Continental Congress, 34–35
slavery, 41
Stamp Act of 1765, 31

T

taxes, 29, 31
Treaty of Paris, 40

U

University of Pennsylvania, 23
US Constitution, 41, 43